EASTER JOKES FOR KIDS

ORCHARD

ORCHARD BOOKS

First published in Great Britain in 2024 by Hodder & Stoughton

1 3 5 7 9 10 8 6 4 2

A CIP catalogue record for this book
is available from the British Library.

ISBN 978 1 40837 389 7

Printed and bound in Great Britain by
Clays Ltd, Elcograf S.p.A

The paper and board used in this book
are made from wood from responsible sources.

MIX
Paper | Supporting
responsible forestry
FSC® C104740
FSC
www.fsc.org

Orchard Books
An imprint of
Hachette Children's Group
Part of Hodder & Stoughton Limited
Carmelite House
50 Victoria Embankment
London EC4Y 0DZ

An Hachette UK Company
www.hachette.co.uk

www.hachettechildrens.co.uk

OVER **300** JOKES

EASTER JOKES FOR KIDS

Elle Owell

Do you know any good Easter egg jokes?

Yeah. I've got a dozen of them!

I was going to tell you a
joke about an Easter egg

... but it's not all it's cracked up to be.

What's the opposite of Easter?

West-er

5

Why was it a surprise the Easter bunny showed up to Easter on time this year?

Because he's always choco-late.

Why were the chickens huddled together?

They were hatching a plan for the Easter egg hunt.

6

Where do lambs go on holiday?

Baaa-rcelona.

Where else do lambs go on holiday?

Baaa-bados.

Why don't rabbits get hot in the summer?

They have hare conditioning.

How do you kiss in spring?

With tu-lips!

What do rabbits say before they eat?

Lettuce pray.

What flowers are the silliest?

Daft-o-dils.

How does the Easter bunny leave
a building in a hurry?

He uses the emergency eggs-it!

When do astronauts
eat their Easter
dinner?

At launch time.

Why can't a rabbit's nose be twelve inches long?

Because then it would be a foot.

Why did the chicken cross the playground?

To get to the other slide!

Where does the Easter bunny live?

Nobunny knows.

What do you call a lamb covered in chocolate?

A candy baa!

Why did the bunnies go on strike?

Because they wanted a better celery.

Why did the Easter bunny fail his driving test?

He liked to egg-celerate too much.

Why was the Easter bunny upset?

He was having a bad hare day.

Why are rabbits so lucky?

They have four rabbit's feet.

How many lambs does it take to knit a jumper?

Don't be silly, lambs can't knit.

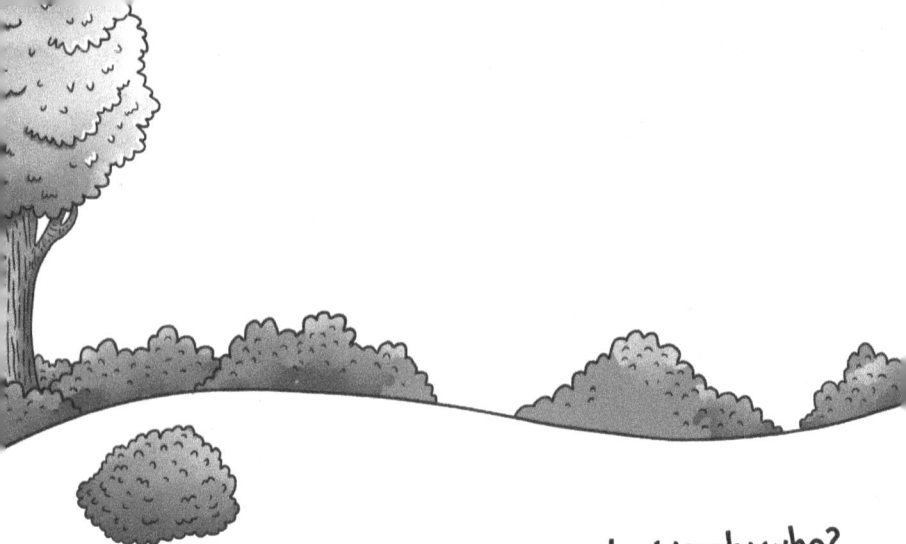

Knock, knock. Who's there? Wendy. Wendy who?
Wendy Easter egg hunt gonna start?

Why did the fox chase the rabbit?
She fancied some fast food.

How many eggs can you put
in an empty Easter basket?
Only one. After that, it's not empty any more.

Knock, knock!
Who's there?
Arthur.
Arthur who?

Arthur any more
Easter eggs to eat?

What do you get if you cross a frog with a rabbit?

A bunny ribbit.

Did you hear about the
scary Easter movie?

It was really hare-raising.

How does the
Easter bunny leave?
He makes an eggs-it.

How does a chick dress for Easter Sunday?
Im-peck-ably.

Why did the Easter bunny fail?
He put all his eggs in one basket.

What do you call an
Easter egg on a safari?

An eggs-plorer.

What do you get when you
cross a bunny with an onion?

A bunion.

Why wasn't the Easter bunny that funny this Easter?

Because someone poached all his best yolks!

15

Why couldn't the Easter bunny watch his favourite show?
Because his TV signal was scrambled.

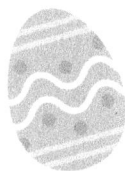

How does the Easter bunny stay fit?
Hare-obics.

Why was the lamb pulled over by police?
She did an illegal ewe turn.

Where do rabbits go after their wedding?

On their bunnymoon.

Did you hear about the man who ate a hundred Easter eggs?

It was egg-cessive.

Where does Dracula keep his Easter eggs?

In his Easter casket!

What do Easter chicks have to do
before they can become hens?

Pass their eggs-ams.

How does a chick always end a date?

With a peck on the cheek.

How long do chicks
like to party?

Around the cluck.

Why do you need an Easter egg hunting license?
Because no poaching is allowed.

What does a mummy egg
say to a baby egg on Easter?
You're eggs-tra special.

How does the Easter bunny deliver
so many Easter eggs on time?
He uses the eggs-press lane!

Why was the little girl sad after the Easter egg hunt?
Because an egg beater!

Did you hear about the dirty Easter egg hunt?
It was hosted by the dust bunny.

What's the Easter bunny's favourite game?
Hopscotch.

What was wrong with the Easter party on the moon?
It had no atmosphere.

Why did the chick
jump up and down?

She was egg-cited
for Easter.

What do you call an Easter
egg from outer space?

An eggs-traterrestrial.

Why don't you see dinosaurs at Easter?

Because they are eggs-tinct.

What do you say to the Easter bunny on his birthday?

Hoppy birthday.

What do you call a sheep that does karate?

Lamb chop.

When is the best time to eat Easter eggs?

At the crack of dawn.

What's a baby chick's favourite game?

Beak-a-boo.

Where does the Easter bunny get his eyes checked?

The hop-ticians.

What made the Easter bunny laugh?

He heard a funny yolk.

What do you call two lambs who are dating?

A relationsheep.

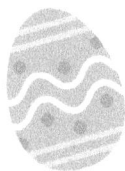

Why did the Easter bunny cross the road?

Because the chicken had his eggs.

Why did the Easter bunny put a dictionary in his trousers?

He wanted to be a smarty pants.

How do you know a rabbit is in a good mood?

She's hoppy.

How did the Easter bunny know he'd eaten too many Easter eggs?

He was feeling hop-eractive.

How can you tell which rabbits are getting old?

Look for the grey hares.

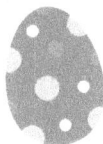

25

Knock, knock! Who's there? Boo. Boo who? Don't cry, Easter will be back next year!

Knock, knock! Who's there?
Some bunny. Some bunny who?
Some bunny's been eating all my Easter chocolate!

What does the Easter bunny read before bed?
Bunny tales.

What do you call a chocolate bunny in the desert?

Hot chocolate.

How do you know an egg is happy?

Its sunny side is up.

What did the magician say after the rabbit vanished?

Hare today, gone tomorrow.

What country does the
Easter bunny live in?
Eggland.

Why was the Easter
egg so strict?
It was hard-boiled.

What do you get if you cross the Easter
bunny with a famous French general?
Napoleon Bunnyparte!

What does an angry rabbit do?

It goes hopping mad.

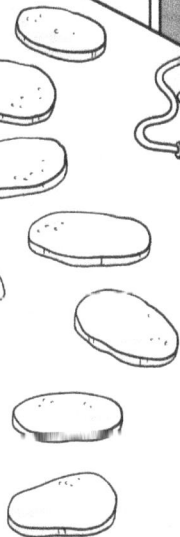

Why are dark chocolate eggs rude?

They think they're bitter than everyone else.

29

What do lambs do to relax at the spa?

They go to the hot wool pool.

Why are Easter eggs bad losers?

They don't like being beaten.

What's invisible and smells of carrots?

Rabbit farts.

Why was the lamb shy?
She was sheepish.

What's the Easter bunny's favourite hot drink?
An eggs-presso coffee.

What do Easter eggs drive?
An egg car-ton.

What do you call a forgetful rabbit?
A hare-brain.

Why don't chocolate bunnies feel any emotions?

They are hollow on the inside.

Why was the Easter bunny arrested?

For hare-assment.

What does the Easter bunny get for making a basket?

Two points, like everyone else!

What do you call a zen egg?
An ommmmmmmelette.

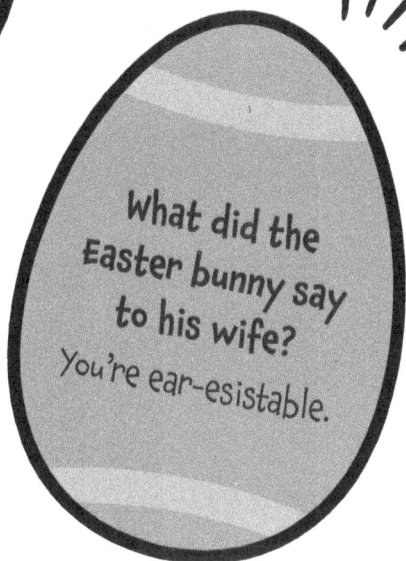

What did the Easter bunny say to his wife?
You're ear-esistable.

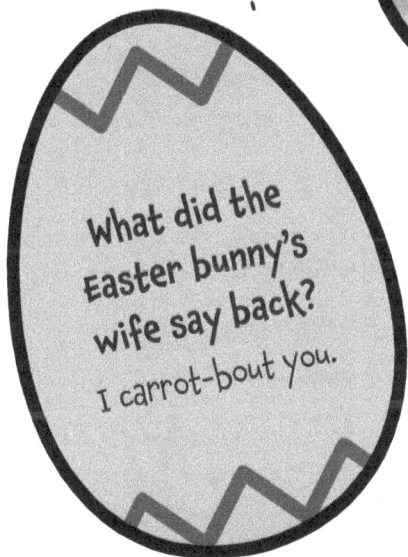

What did the Easter bunny's wife say back?
I carrot-bout you.

33

What do you call a sleepy Easter egg?

Eggs-hausted.

Where do Easter
farts come from?

The Easter bummy.

How do you make a rabbit stew?

Make it wait for three hours.

How do you send a
letter to the Easter bunny?

By hare mail.

How do rabbits travel?

By hare-plane.

What side of the Easter bunny has the most fur?

The outside.

What happens if you fall in love on Easter?

You live hoppily ever after.

What do you call a dancing chick?

Poultry in motion.

Why was the egg hiding?

It was chicken.

Where should you look for treasure on Easter?

Wherever eggs marks the spot.

Why did the
Easter bunny love
the chocolate bunny?

Because she was so sweet.

How does the Easter
bunny keep his fur
looking so nice?

He uses hare spray.

**How does the Easter bunny deliver
all those eggs in one night?**
I don't know, but it's probably Easter said than done.

**Why is the Easter bunny
so good at his job?**
He has lots of eggs-perience.

What do you call a daffodil that glows in the dark?
A light bulb.

**Why was the
Easter egg green?**
It was mint
to be eaten.

How does the Easter bunny
paint all those Easter eggs?
He hires Santa's elves to help
during their off-season.

Why did the Easter bunny have to fire the duck?
Because she kept quacking the eggs.

How many Easter eggs can
you find at an Easter egg hunt?
A choco-lot!

39

What do you say after you burp during your Easter dinner?

Eggs-cuse me!

How should you wish Easter greetings to a rabbit?

Say Hoppy Easter.

How do you tame a wild hare?

Wear an Easter bonnet.

What did the egg say after passing its test?

Omelette smarter than I look.

What do you call an island filled with Easter eggs?

A dessert island.

What do you get when you pour warm water into a rabbit hole?

Hot, cross bunnies.

41

Why did the lamb crash the car?

Because she was a sheep at the wheel.

What is the opposite of a chocolate bunny?

A choco-early bunny.

What does the Easter bunny eat for lunch?

Easter egg salad.

Why were the Easter eggs running so fast?

They were afraid of being beaten.

**Why were the
two lambs so close?**

They had a great friendsheep.

**What do you call a chocolate
bunny that's been out in
the sun too long?**

A runny bunny.

**Why are people tired
at Easter in April?**

Because they just
finished a March.

**Why wasn't the lamb
allowed in the meadow?**

She had a gambolling problem.

Why are bunnies so lazy?
Because they don't carrot all.

What do lambs sing on birthdays?
Happy birthday to ewe.

What kind of hotel rooms do chocolate bunnies reserve?
Sweets.

Why are March, April
and May the hoppiest
times of the year?

Everyone has a
spring in their step.

What happens to misbehaving
Easter eggs at school?

They get eggs-pelled.

What's an Easter
egg's favourite
kind of party?

One that's choco-lit!

Why doesn't the Easter bunny celebrate Halloween?
It's too hare-raising.

How does the Easter bunny stay safe?
He's got a bunny guard.

What's the Easter bunny's favourite sandwich filling?
Easter egg mayonnaise.

Why couldn't the Easter bunny sleep on Easter eve?
He was too egg-cited.

What did one Easter egg say to the other?

Have an eggs-tra special day!

Why is the Easter bunny so funny?

He always has a tail to tell.

What do you call a happy rabbit?

A hop-timist.

What did the thief say when she was caught stealing Easter eggs?

I can eggs-plain!

What do bunnies say when they come home from work?

Anybunny home?

What do you call an Easter bunny wearing a kilt?

Hopscotch.

The Easter bunny joined the Olympics.

He heard first place gets twenty-four carrots.

What's a bunny's favourite type of book?

One with a hoppy ending.

What do you get when you cross a rabbit with a shellfish?

An oyster bunny.

What kind of bunny can't hop?

A chocolate one.

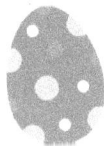

49

Did you hear about the chick's Easter party?
It was a shell of a time.

Why don't chicks
play baseball?
Too many fowl balls.

What did one chocolate egg say to the other?
You're sweet.

What did the eggs do
when the traffic light
turned green?
They egg-celerated.

Why did the hen ask the rooster out on a date?
She was feeling plucky.

Did you hear about the chick that went to jail?
The police suspected fowl play.

What did the little lamb
say to her mum?
I love ewe.

What's the Easter bunny's favourite drink?
Hop chocolate.

Why are hot cross
buns perfect for Easter?
They rise to the occasion.

Why did the chick
need a holiday?
She was feeling cooped out.

Did you hear about the Easter bunny's wedding?
The ring was made of fourteen-carrot gold.

Did you hear about the girl who nearly hit the Easter bunny with her bike?

She missed him by a hare.

What happened when a thousand hares got loose in the city?

The police had to comb the area.

Where does Christmas come before Easter?

The dictionary.

Did you hear about the Easter bunny's broken leg?
It had a hare-line fracture.

What do you get when you cross an angry lamb with an angry cow?
An animal in a very baaaaad moooood.

Why doesn't anyone want to be an Easter egg?
Because they're always dye-ing.

What do Easter eggs do when they're scared?
Scramble.

What did one Easter
egg say to the other?
Heard any good yolks today?

Where do rabbits learn how to fly planes?
The Royal Hare Force.

What city has the
most Easter eggs?
New Yolk City.

Knock, knock. Who's there?
Shirley. Shirley who?
Shirley you can't eat all those
Easter eggs. Let me help you.

Why do hens lay eggs?
Because if they dropped them, they'd break.

Where's the best place to learn about eggs?
The hen-cyclopedia.

Why shouldn't you tickle an Easter egg?
You don't want it to crack up.

What kind of stories do Easter eggs like to tell their children?

Yolk tales.

Where does the Easter bunny go to dance?

The basket-ball.

How do lambs wash?

In the baaath-tub.

What do you call an evil Easter egg?

A devilled egg.

What does the Easter bunny say when he hops through the front door?

Bunny, I'm home.

A chicken and an egg walk into a shop. The shop assistant says, "Which of you is first?"

Why is the Easter bunny a good listener?

He's all ears.

What do you call a bunny with lots of money?
A millionhare.

What day do eggs hate the most?

Fry-day.

What do you call the Easter bunny when Easter is over?

Eggs-hausted.

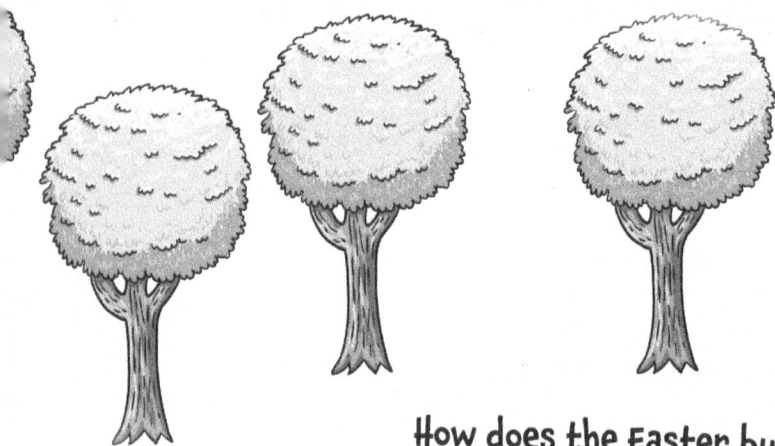

How does the Easter bunny
deliver all the Easter eggs on time?

He just hops to it.

Where did the lamb
end up after she
robbed the farmer?

Behind baaas.

Knock, knock! Who's there?
Police. Police who?

Police hurry up and
decorate your eggs.

Why can the Easter
bunny hop so high?

Because he was
born in spring.

Knock, knock! Who's there? Some bunny.
Some bunny who?
Some bunny's been hiding my Easter eggs!

How do you make an egg roll?
Just give it a little push.

What sport are eggs best at?

Running.

What do chicks
do on Easter?

Eat chocolate
around the cluck.

How does the Easter bunny dry his fur?

With a hare dryer.

What's the best way to make Easter easier?

Put an "i" where the "t" is.

Why did the bald man put the Easter bunny on his head?

Because from a distance it looked like hare.

What is the Easter bunny's favourite kind of music?

Hip-hop!

What's an egg's favourite tree?

The might-y-oak!

What do you get if you cross a bunny with a tennis court?

A hare-net.

What do you get if you cross a bunny with a leaf blower?

Hare-raising wind!

Why are Easter eggs such bad comedians?

They always mix up their yokes.

Where do lambs get their wool cut?

The baa-baa.

What's the Easter bunny's favourite sweet treat?

Millionhare shortbread.

What animals are scared of vacuum cleaners?

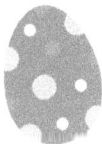

Dust bunnies.

What did the farmer
say to the sad lamb?

Shear up!

What do you call
a snugly rabbit?

Hugs bunny.

What happened to the
egg after it went on
the rollercoaster?

It was scrambled.

What's the difference between a rabbit at the gym and a rabbit with a carrot on her head?

One's a fit bunny, the other's a bit funny.

What do you get when you cross a bumblebee with a rabbit?

A honey bunny.

How can you make Easter faster?

Replace the 'E' with an 'F'.

I went to eat my Easter egg,
but I couldn't find it anywhere.

I think someone must've poached it.

Did you hear about the woman who
complained about her rabbit stew?

She said there was a hare in her soup.

What did the hen say to her naughty child?

You're such a rotten egg!

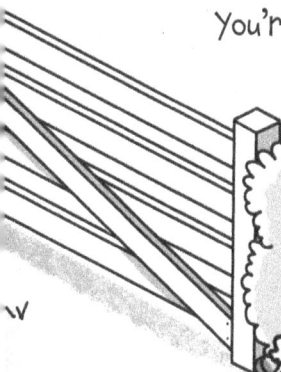

How does the Easter bunny stay fit?

Eggs-ercise.

What did the Easter bunny say to his best friend?
Nobunny compares to you.

What do you call an exploding Easter egg?
A bombshell.

What do you say to someone who couldn't find any eggs at an egg hunt?
Looks like you're fresh outta cluck.

Why is the Easter bunny so good at his job?
Because he's an Easter eggs-pert.

I only had five minutes to season
the Easter dinner before it went in the oven.
It was a race against thyme.

What do you call a scared egg?
Terri-fried.

Who tells the best eggs puns?
The comedi-hens!

Where can you find
Easter eggs in the Arctic?
Inside egg-loos.

Why do rabbits have long ears?
To cover their lack of hares.

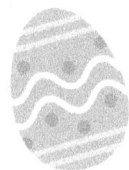

Why did the celebrity Easter egg start losing its friends?
They called it a shell-out.

What did one tulip say to the other?
How's it growing?

What do you call a mischievous Easter egg?

A practical yolker.

How do you know when it's too hot in the chicken barn?

The hens start laying hard-boiled eggs.

Why do eggs go to school?

To get egg-ducated.

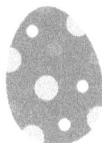

How do Easter eggs grow?

From an eggplant.

What did the Easter bunny say to the carrot?

It's been nice growing you.

What are gegs?

Scrambled eggs.

How do comedians like their Easter eggs?
Funny side up!

What did the Easter bunny say to the other carrot?
It's been nice gnawing you.

I know a good joke about a lamb.

Stop me if you've herd it before.

Where do rabbits go when they are feeling sick?
To the hop-spital.

What did the veterinarian say to the Easter bunny?
A carrot a day keeps the doctors away.

Why was the Easter bunny feeling unwell?
Because he had an egg-ache.

Where do tough chickens come from?
Hard-boiled eggs.

How does the Easter bunny like to travel?

On a Seggway.

What do you call a quiet lamb?

A shhheep.

What does a chicken consider the perfect Easter date?

A peck-nic in the park.

What did the chick say at the end of the Easter egg hunt?

That's all, yolks.

One Easter I ate all my
Easter eggs in one sitting.
No eggrets!

How many Easter eggs does it
take to screw in a light bulb?
None. Easter eggs don't have hands.

What fruit loves Easter chocolate?
A cocoa-nut.

What do you get if you
cross a lamb and a rocket?
A space sheep.

Why do we paint Easter eggs?

Because it's easier than wallpapering them.

What do you call a row of rabbits jumping backwards?

A receding hare-line.

Why are Easter egg jokes so funny?

Because they crack you up.

If a rooster laid an egg on top of a hill, which side would it roll down?

Neither – roosters don't lay eggs.

What's a lamb's favourite song?
Anything by Lady Baa Baa.

What did the lamb say to the other?
Ewe are one in a million.

Why is the Easter bunny so smart?
He's an egghead!

Where does the Easter bunny go when he needs a new tail?

To a re-tail store!

Knock, knock.
Who's there?
Easter. Easter who?
The Easter bunny, who else would be knocking?

How do you turn a white chocolate egg into a dark chocolate egg?

Just turn off the lights.

What do you call chocolate bunny poo?
Chocolate sprinkles!

How does a barista take their coffee at Easter?
Eggs-tra strong!

What do you call an unconventional Easter egg?
Egg-centric.

Why should you be careful what you say about egg whites?

They can't take a yolk.

How did the detective find out the chicken came before the egg?

She looked it up in the dictionary.

What do you call a dancing lamb?

A baaallerina.

Knock, knock.
Who's there?
You. You who?

Yoo-hoo! Time to hop over to the egg hunt.

What did two Easter eggs say when they bumped into each other?

Eggs-cuse me.

Why was the Easter bunny studying the Easter egg?

He was trying to decide which came first, the chocolate chicken or the chocolate egg!

What did the hen say when she got a new Easter bonnet?

Chick me out!

Knock, knock. Who's there? Who. Who who?

Today's about bunnies, not owls.

I accidentally drank the water we used to colour eggs for Easter.

I think I dyed a little inside.

Why was the Easter bunny so annoying?
He kept rabbiting on.

How does the Easter bunny keep his fur looking good?
With a hare-brush!

Would February March?
No, but April May!

Where do naughty Easter eggs go?

A corr-egg-tional facility.

What's red and blue and sogs
up your Easter basket?

Scrambled Easter eggs!

How did the Easter
bunny rate his
chocolate?

Egg-cellent.

Did you hear about the
determined lamb?

Where there's a wool,
there's a way!

What do you call a rabbit with fleas?

Bugs bunny.

What is the Easter bunny's favourite dance?

The bunny hop!

Did you hear about the lady whose house was overrun with Easter eggs?

She had to call an eggs-terminator.

What did the Easter bunny say to cheer people up?

Don't worry, be hoppy.

Why did the rabbit cross the road?

Because it was the chicken's day off.

What has big ears, brings Easter treats, and goes "hippity-BOOM, hippity-BOOM, hippity-BOOM"?

The Easter elephant.

Why is a rabbit similar to a coin?

Because it has a head on one end and a tail on the other.

What has long ears, four legs and is worn on your head?

An Easter bunnet.

What do Easter eggs do for fun?

Kar-ee-yolk-e!

How did the chicks make sure they were on time for Easter morning?

They used an alarm cluck.

What do you call a half price bunch of daffodils?

A daffodeal.

It's true that bunnies have good eyesight . . .

You never see a bunny wearing glasses, after all!

What is the difference between a fake bank note and an angry bunny?

One is bad money and the other is a mad bunny.

What's long and stylish and full of cats?

The Easter purrade.

Where does the Easter bunny live?

Just a hop, a skip and a jump away.

What do you get when you cross a rabbit with an elephant?

An animal who never forgets to eat its carrots.

Why are flowers never lonely in spring?
They have lots of buds.

Where can you watch cute lamb videos?
EweTube.

Did you hear the one about the Easter bunny who sat on a bee?
It's a tender tail.

What is the Easter bunny's favourite sport?
Easter basket-ball!

How do you make friends with an Easter egg?

You gotta get it out of its shell.

Why did the Easter egg hide?

It was a little chicken.

What looks like half an Easter egg?

The other half.

How do you get a rabbit to do what you want?
With a carrot-and-stick approach.

What do you need if your chocolate eggs mysteriously disappear?
An eggs-planation.

How did the Easter egg get up the hill?
It scrambled up.

93

What do you call a rabbit who makes good jokes?

A funny bunny.

What do you get when you cross a lamb with a computer?

RAM.

What's yellow, has long ears and grows on trees?

The Easter bunana.

Where does the Easter bunny go to trim his fur?

The hare-dresser.

Why did the chicken run out of the coop?

It smelled like a rotten egg!

Want some good Easter advice?

Don't put all your eggs in one basket.

What kind of stories do Easter bunnies like best?

Hare-y tales.

What do you say to your parents before you go to bed on Easter?

Nobunny touch my chocolate!

More hilarious joke books coming soon ...

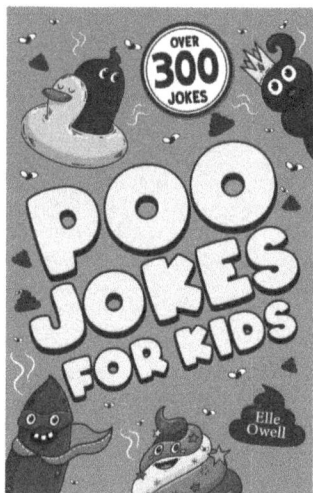

POO JOKES FOR KIDS

OVER 300 JOKES

Elle Owell

SPOOKY JOKES FOR KIDS

OVER 300 JOKES

Elle Owell

CHRISTMAS JOKES FOR KIDS

OVER 300 JOKES